ANDY GOLDSWORTHY

ENDPAPERS

Ends of bamboo
pushed into bitten holes to make screen
growing dark
calm, warm, humid, raining, mosquitoes

KIINAGASHIMA-CHO, JAPAN
27 NOVEMBER 1987

OVERLEAF

Dandelions
newly flowered
none as yet turned to seed
undamaged by wind or rain
a grass verge between dual carriageways

NEAR WEST BRETTON, YORKSHIRE
28 APRIL 1987

ANDY GOLDSWORTHY

VIKING

VIKING

Published by the Penguin Group
Penguin Books Ltd, 27 Wrights Lane, London W8 5TZ, England
Penguin Books USA Inc., 375 Hudson Street, New York, New York 10014, USA
Penguin Books Australia Ltd, Ringwood, Victoria, Australia
Penguin Books Canada Ltd, 10 Alcorn Avenue, Toronto, Ontario, Canada M4V 3B2
Penguin Books (NZ) Ltd, 182–190 Wairau Road, Auckland 10, New Zealand

Penguin Books Ltd, Registered Offices: Harmondsworth, Middlesex, England

First published 1990

10 9 8 7

Produced by Jill Hollis and Ian Cameron for Cameron Books, Moffat, Dumfriesshire, Scotland

Filmset in Gill Sans Light

Printed in Italy by Artegrafica, Verona
A CIP catalogue record for this book is available from the British Library

ISBN 0-670-83213-8

Andy Goldsworthy is represented by the Fabian Carlsson Gallery, London

I should like to thank Ian Cameron and Jill Hollis, the Fabian Carlsson Gallery, Clive Adams and Dr
Terry Friedman of the Henry Moore Centre for the Study of Sculpture. I also wish to thank my wife
Judith who assisted in the making and photographing of several works in this book. The earthworks
were commissioned by Sustrans Ltd and Northern Arts.   A. G.

Sweet chestnut green horn
continuous spiral
each leaf laid in the fold of another
stitched with thorns.

YORKSHIRE SCULPTURE PARK, WEST BRETTON
9 AUGUST 1987

INTRODUCTION

For me, looking, touching, material, place and form are all inseparable from the resulting work. It is difficult to say where one stops and another begins. Place is found by walking, direction determined by weather and season. I take the opportunities each day offers: if it is snowing, I work with snow, at leaf-fall it will be with leaves; a blown-over tree becomes a source of twigs and branches.

I stop at a place or pick up a material because I feel that there is something to be discovered. Here is where I can learn. I might have walked past or worked there many times. Some places I return to over and over again, going deeper — a relationship made in layers over a long time. Staying in one place makes me more aware of change. I might give up after a while. My perception of a place is often so frustratingly limited. The best of my work, sometimes the result of much struggle when made, appears so obvious that it is incredible I didn't see it before. It was there all the time.

Movement, change, light, growth and decay are the lifeblood of nature, the energies that I try to tap through my work. I need the shock of touch, the resistance of place, materials and weather, the earth as my source. I want to get under the surface. When I work with a leaf, rock, stick, it is not just that material in itself, it is an opening into the processes of life within and around it. When I leave it, these processes continue.

The energy and space around a material are as important as the energy and space within. The weather — rain, sun, snow, hail, mist, calm — is that external space made visible. When I touch a rock, I am touching and working the space around it. It is not independent of its surroundings and the way it sits tells how it came to be there. In an effort to understand why that rock is there and where it is going, I must work with it in the area in which I found it.

I have become aware of how nature is in a state of change and how that change is the key to understanding. I want my art to be sensitive and alert to changes in material, season and weather. Often I can only follow a train of thought while a particular weather condition persists. When a change comes, the idea must alter or it will, and often does, fail. I am sometimes left stranded by a change in the weather with half-understood feelings that have to travel with me until conditions are right for them to reappear.

During the one persistently cold period that I have had to work with in Britain I was able to pursue ideas only hinted at in previous winters. It is difficult to predict where good ice and icicles will form. In summer I saw potential in the dripping walls and small pools at Glenmarlin Falls on the River Scaur in Dumfriesshire.

When the cold arrived, that is where I went — disappointed at first because it was too sheltered by overhanging trees. One small pool was barely frozen. I used this precious ice — the work was not good, but it gave me a feel for the place.

As winter progressed, it became colder. Different pools started to freeze on different days, depending on how sheltered they were or whether they were fed by running water (these pools were the last to freeze). Always a range of thicknesses to work with – as a pool froze solid and became unworkable, I moved on to the next.

I worked in the shadow of the gorge where the sun only reached for a dangerous half hour each day. In this cold shade I tentatively began to stick ice to ice to icicle to rock – making works in pairs – going from one to the other – giving time for each new piece of ice to freeze.

As the cold intensified, my work became more ambitious and demanding – one work a day, with the ice sticking in just a few minutes. What had taken days in previous winters was now being made in a single day. I cannot explain the feelings of that short time – working the cold, hot with excitement.

What I learned that week went beyond the ice in my hand. It was as if the previous twelve years' work had prepared me for such a place – work-bench rocks, a pool to hand in which to dip ice before freezing it to the work, sheltered from sun and wind, the fast-flowing salmon river, geese flying overhead in a V, otter tracks on the ice below ...

When I work with winter, I work with the North. For me, north is an integral part of the land. I can touch it in the cold shadow of a mountain, the green side of a tree, the mossy face of a rock. Its energy is made visible in snow and ice.

I have followed north to its source – the North Pole – the place from which winter is generated. Going there has given me a better understanding not only of the nature of winter and north but also of the place where I live. I enjoyed the luxury of constant freezing. So much that I have made in ice has been frustrated by a rise in temperature. I have held ice to ice seemingly for ages waiting for it to freeze, only to let go and see it drop off.

Working in Britain means working close to change: a clear day can soon cloud over, snow melts quickly, a calm morning turns windy. These qualities give urgency and energy to what I do.

Sometimes a work is at its best when most threatened by the weather. A balanced rock is given enormous tension and force by a wind that might cause its collapse. I have worked with colourful leaves, delicate grasses and feathers made extra vivid by a dark, rain-laden sky that cast no shadow. Had it rained, the work would have become mud-splattered and been washed away.

Each work concentrates on a particular aspect of material and place. The grass stalk is hard, brittle, hollow and fractures at angles; the seed-head is supple, thin, strong, whippy. It takes many works to come to some understanding of 'stalk', let alone 'grass', and the process never stops. Should I ignore the geometry in grass stalks fractured by the wind?

All forms are to be found in nature, and there are many qualities within any material. By exploring them I hope to understand the whole. My work needs to include the loose and disordered within the nature of material as well as the tight and regular.

1985 saw my first use of the spiral. It took me a long time to come to terms with this form, so evident in nature, and I still avoid the overblown spiral. I prefer that of the unfolding fern, which gives the feeling of endless growth.

The ball, patch, line, arch and spire are recurring forms in my work. It is as if I find myself in deep water and these forms are familiar rocks that I can always put a foot to. In that respect they are important and probably necessary. They are also an effective way of exploring and extending a work over time, materials and locations.

The hole has become an important element. Looking into a deep hole unnerves me. My concept of stability is questioned and I am made aware of the potent energies within the earth. The black is that energy made visible.

Recurring forms are discovered in unlikely materials. Snow becomes as sand, rock as ice. One teaches me about another and gives an understanding of the qualities that are fundamental to the way nature functions.

Some works have qualities of snaking but are not snakes. The form is shaped through a similar response to environment. The snake has evolved through a need to move close to the ground, sometimes below and sometimes above, an expression of the space it occupies. This is a potent recurring form in nature which I have explored through working in bracken, snow, sand, leaves, grass, trees, earth. It is the ridge of a mountain, the root of a tree, a river finding its way down a valley.

At its most successful, my 'touch' looks into the heart of nature; most days I don't even get close. These things are all part of a transient process that I cannot understand unless my touch is also transient – only in this way can the cycle remain unbroken and the process be complete. I cannot explain the importance to me of being part of a place, its seasons and changes. Fourteen years ago I made a line of stones in Morecambe Bay. It is still there, buried under the sand, unseen. All my work still exists, in some form.

My approach to the photograph is kept simple, almost routine. All work, good and bad, is documented. I use standard film, a standard lens and no filters.

Each work grows, stays, decays – integral parts of a cycle which the photograph shows at its height, marking the moment when the work is most alive. There is an intensity about a work at its peak that I hope is expressed in the image. Process and decay are implicit.

That art should be permanent or impermanent is not the issue. Transience in my work reflects what I find in nature and should not be confused with an attitude towards art generally. I have never been against the well-made or long-lasting.

Of course there are opposites and conflicts in my work, uncomfortable though creative tensions, which I use to sharpen my relationship with nature. I refuse to resolve them prematurely to make my own position easier. Discomfort is a sign of change. Every so often I feel as birds must before their first migration – a gut instinct that something is wrong where they are, a strong sense that they must now go where they have never been before. The one contradiction I won't tolerate is having an art that binds me.

I need to work in a wide range of scale, reflecting what I find in nature. Working small with grasses or leaves is a strain. A sudden gust, a hungry robin, even a worm can cause collapse. I enjoy these delicate tensions, but they cause an occasional need to work large and physically hard. One scale releases energy for the other.

My approach to larger, more permanent work is longer-term. There is a process of familiarisation with site through drawings that explore the location and the space. This is the only time I use drawing to work through ideas; for me it represents a change in approach. I often live with a site at the back of my mind for months, sometimes years – a target for energies and ideas.

I dislike gigantism for its own sake, but small works can grow into large. By this I don't mean a coarse scaling-up, but a maturing and development of forms and feelings – often in only one material, or rediscovered in another, changing during the process. This is not planned, it happens over years.

By working large, I am not trying to dominate nature. If people feel small in relation to a work, they should not assume that there is an intention to make nature itself small. If anything, I am giving nature a more powerful presence in the mass of earth, stone, wood that I use. I do not change the underlying processes of growth, and nature's grip is tightened on the site that I have worked.

The earthworks in County Durham are made along the route of a disused railway line which I have begun to see as a river of earth. If the Lambton Earthwork is made on a fast-flowing part of the line, then at Leadgate the earth has formed a deep pool, dammed by the road. The rings are as ripples from a thrown stone – an echo of a maze formed by the coal-mining directly below it, deep down.

The social nature of these large works interests me. The people I need to work with are a strong element in the making. New demands can provoke creative solutions.

I have been given a small piece of woodland in Dumfriesshire by the Buccleuch Estates. I call this place Stonewood. Part of the lease required me to build a dividing wall. I have made a give-and-take wall between the farmer and myself. Two sheep folds are incorporated into the wall: one opening on the farmer's side for sheep, one opening on my side for sculpture. The sheep will in effect be on my land and the sculpture on the farmer's.

The work itself determines the nature of its making. I enjoy the freedom of just using my hands and 'found' tools – a sharp stone, the quill of a feather, thorns. I am not playing the primitive. I use my hands because this is the best way to do most of my work. If I need tools, then I will use them. Technology, travel and tools are part of my life and if needed should be part of my work also. A camera is used to document, an excavator to move earth, snowballs are carried cross country by articulated truck.

Nature goes beyond what is called countryside – everything comes from the earth. My work made indoors or with urban and industrial materials is an attempt to discover nature in these things also. It is more difficult to find nature in materials so far removed from their source, and I cannot go for long before I need to work with the earth direct – hand to earth. What is important to me is that at the heart of whatever I do are a growing understanding and a sharpening perception of the land.

Dandelion flowers
pinned with thorns to wind-bent willowherb stalks
laid in a ring
held above bluebells with forked sticks

YORKSHIRE SCULPTURE PARK, WEST BRETTON
1 MAY 1987

Elder leaves

BROUGH, CUMBRIA
1 SEPTEMBER 1981

Cherry leaves

SWINDALE BECK WOOD, CUMBRIA
NOVEMBER 1984

Poplar leaves

PENPONT, DUMFRIESSHIRE
7 NOVEMBER 1986

Rosebay willowherb leaves

SWINDALE BECK WOOD, CUMBRIA
OCTOBER 1981

Rotten alder wood

HELBECK, CUMBRIA
NOVEMBER 1983

Rotten birch wood

BROUGH, CUMBRIA
MAY 1984

Line and cairn to follow colours in pebbles

ST ABBS, THE BORDERS
31 MAY & 1 JUNE 1985

Rowan leaves laid around hole
collecting the last few leaves
nearly finished
dog ran into hole
started again
made in the shade on a windy, sunny day

YORKSHIRE SCULPTURE PARK, WEST BRETTON
25 OCTOBER 1987

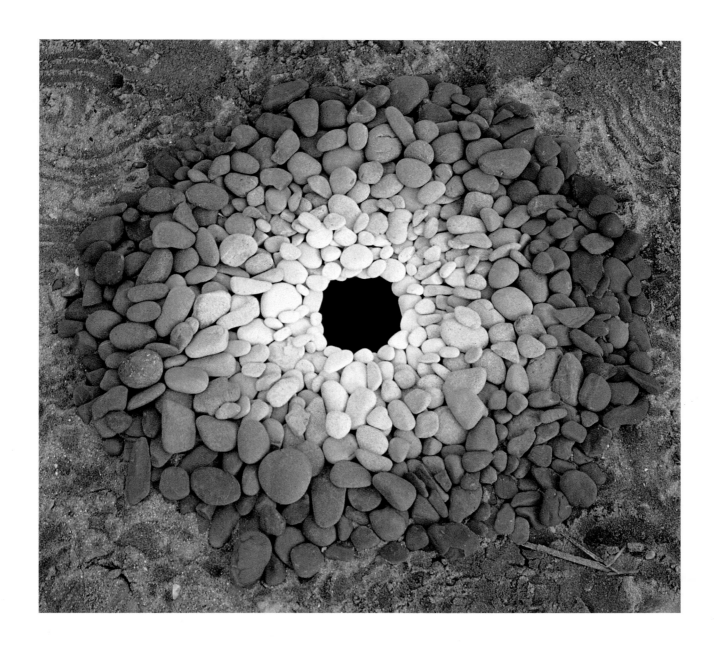

Pebbles around a hole

KIINAGASHIMA-CHO, JAPAN
7 DECEMBER 1987

Leaves on leaves
pressed flat with spit
held to ground with stalks and thorns
windy

YORKSHIRE SCULPTURE PARK, WEST BRETTON
22 OCTOBER 1987

Bramble leaves

turning colour

HAMPSTEAD HEATH, LONDON

20 DECEMBER 1985

Dug trench
edged with clay
supported with sticks

YORKSHIRE SCULPTURE PARK
WEST BRETTON
6-7 AUGUST 1987

Slate crack line

LITTLE LANGDALE, CUMBRIA
FEBRUARY 1988

Leaves
torn in two
pressed to the ground with mud
leaving a gap

GLASGOW GREEN
2 NOVEMBER 1986

Broken pebbles

SCAUR WATER, DUMFRIESSHIRE
12 APRIL 1987

Broken stones
scratched white

MORECAMBE BAY, LANCASHIRE
JANUARY 1978

Oak leaves in holes

ILKLEY, YORKSHIRE
1978

Bracken

BORROWDALE, CUMBRIA
13 FEBRUARY 1988

Driftwood

KIINAGASHIMA-CHO, JAPAN
29 NOVEMBER 1987

Slate

STONEWOOD, DUMFRIESSHIRE
SUMMER 1987

Plane leaves

CASTRES, FRANCE
19 OCTOBER 1988

Torn hole
horse chestnut leaves stitched with stalks around the rim
moving in the wind

CAMBRIDGE
24 JULY 1986

Damp sand
hollowed out
soft red stone ground into powder round each hole

ISLE OF WIGHT
JUNE 1987

Fine dry sand
edges and ridges
softened by the breeze

ARIZONA
21 NOVEMBER 1989

Continuous grass stalk lines
each stalk pushed into the wider hollow end of another
or two thin ends joined with a short length of thicker stalk
edging a hole, climbing a tree
pinned with thorns

YORKSHIRE SCULPTURE PARK, WEST BRETTON & HELBECK, CUMBRIA
SEPTEMBER 1983 & MAY 1984

Thin-edged stones
laid around a hollow

CLAPHAM SCAR, YORKSHIRE
JANUARY 1980

Ice arch
left to freeze overnight
before supporting pile of stones removed
(made in a field with cows – a tense wait)
pissed on stones too frozen to come out
fourth attempt successful
other three arches collapsed or melted

BROUGH, CUMBRIA
1-2 DECEMBER 1982

Slate arch
made over two days
fourth attempt

BLAENAU FFESTINIOG, WALES
SEPTEMBER 1982

Slate stack
cracking and shifting as it became heavier

LITTLE LANGDALE, CUMBRIA
JULY 1986

Balanced rocks

SWINDALE BECK WOOD, CUMBRIA
24 SEPTEMBER 1982

IZUMI-MURA, JAPAN
30 DECEMBER 1987

Balanced rock
misty

LANGDALE, CUMBRIA
MAY 1977

Slate thorn

BLAENAU FFESTINIOG, WALES
MAY 1980

Stacked stone

BLAENAU FFESTINIOG, WALES
JUNE 1980

Snowball in trees

ROBERT HALL WOOD, LANCASHIRE
FEBRUARY 1980 .

OVERLEAF

Snowball trail
wet, heavy snow
second attempt
first try driven over by a tractor

BROUGH, CUMBRIA
9 MARCH 1982

Large, fallen oak tree
used leaves with branches still attached
for supporting structure inside ball

JENNY NOBLE'S GILL, DUMFRIESSHIRE
15 SEPTEMBER 1985

Stacked ice
sound of cracking

HAMPSTEAD HEATH, LONDON
28 DECEMBER 1985

Poppy petals
wrapped around a boulder
held with water

SIDOBRE, FRANCE
6 JUNE 1989

Frost

PENPONT, DUMFRIESSHIRE
3 DECEMBER 1989

Sycamore

MIDDLETON WOODS, YORKSHIRE
9 FEBRUARY 1981

Leaf patch edges made by finding leaves the same size
tearing one in two
spitting underneath and pressing flat on to another

Oak

HAMPSTEAD HEATH, LONDON
31 DECEMBER 1985

Elm

MIDDLETON WOODS, YORKSHIRE
7 NOVEMBER 1980

Elm

MIDDLETON WOODS, YORKSHIRE
6 NOVEMBER 1980

Cherry

SWINDALE BECK WOOD, CUMBRIA
4 NOVEMBER 1984

Damp

RIVER WHARF, YORKSHIRE
APRIL 1981

Lichen

IKLEY MOOR, YORKSHIRE
FEBRUARY 1981

Blue pebbles rubbed with red stones to make edge

ST ABBS, THE BORDERS
JUNE 1984

Grey stones rubbed red

HELBECK, CUMBRIA
11 MARCH 1984

Feathers plucked from dead heron
cut with sharp stone
stripped down one side
about three-and-a-half feet overall length
made over three calm days
cold frosty mornings
smell from heron pungent as each day warmed up

SWINDALE BECK WOOD, CUMBRIA
24-26 FEBRUARY 1982

OVERLEAF

Branches stacked over two weeks

HELBECK, CUMBRIA
FEBRUARY 1983

Goose feathers
carefully stripped down one side
bent over and held to the ground with thorns

HELBECK, CUMBRIA
10 JUNE 1983

Woven silver birch

LANGHOLM, DUMFRIESSHIRE
APRIL 1986

Leaves torn between the veins
stitched together with pine needles
hung from a tree
raining, calm, cold

IZUMI-MURA, JAPAN
21 DECEMBER 1987

Slab of snow
carved into
leaving a translucent layer
horse chestnut stalks pinned together with thin bamboo

IZUMI-MURA, JAPAN
27 DECEMBER 1987

Out early to work the cold
a wall of frozen snow
carved with a stick
almost through to the other side
collapsed in the sunlight

IZUMI-MURA, JAPAN
25 DECEMBER 1987

Bright sunny morning
frozen snow
cut slab
scraped snow away with a stick
just short of breaking through

IZUMI-MURA, JAPAN
19 DECEMBER 1987

Hollow snowballs

BLENCATHRA, CUMBRIA
8 FEBRUARY 1988

Slits cut into frozen snow
stormy
strong wind
weather and light rapidly changing

BLENCATHRA, CUMBRIA
12 FEBRUARY 1988

Snow slabs
stood on end
for the wind

30 MARCH 1989

OVERLEAF

Snow spires
Photograph – Julian Calder

GRISE FIORD, ELLESMERE ISLAND
15 APRIL 1989

Touching north
Photograph – Julian Calder

NORTH POLE
24 APRIL 1989

Lay down as it started raining or snowing
waited until the ground became wet or covered before getting up

TEWET TARN, CUMBRIA
5 MARCH 1988

KIINAGASHIMA-CHO, JAPAN
27 NOVEMBER 1987

HAARLEM, HOLLAND
29 AUGUST 1984

TEWET TARN, CUMBRIA
5 MARCH 1988

ST ABBS, THE BORDERS
JUNE 1984

Snow and mud

BROUGH, CUMBRIA
18 JANUARY 1985

Sycamore leaves
one peeled off a cow clap
turned black
one caught in briars
bleached by sun and wind

BENTHAM, YORKSHIRE
MARCH 1980

MIDDLETON WOODS, YORKSHIRE
JANUARY 1981

Sycamore stick placed on snow
raining heavily
snow gone by next day
bark stripped, chewed and scraped off

MIDDLETON WOODS, YORKSHIRE
16-17 JANUARY 1981

Ice and icicles
dipped in water
held against rock and ice until frozen

SCAUR WATER, PENPONT, DUMFRIESSHIRE
7-8 JANUARY 1987

Icicles
thick ends dipped in snow then water
held until frozen together
occasionally using forked sticks as support until stuck
a tense moment when taking them away
breathing on the stick first to release it

SCAUR WATER, DUMFRIESSHIRE
12 JANUARY 1987

Thin ice
made over two days
welded with water from dripping ice
hollow inside

SCAUR WATER, DUMFRIESSHIRE
10-11 JANUARY 1987

Iris blades pinned together with thorns
filled in five sections with rowan berries
fish attacking from below
difficult to keep all the berries in
nibbled at by ducks

YORKSHIRE SCULPTURE PARK, WEST BRETTON
29 AUGUST 1987

Early morning calm
knotweed stalks
pushed into lake bottom
made complete by their own reflections

DERWENT WATER, CUMBRIA
20 FEBRUARY & 8-9 MARCH 1988

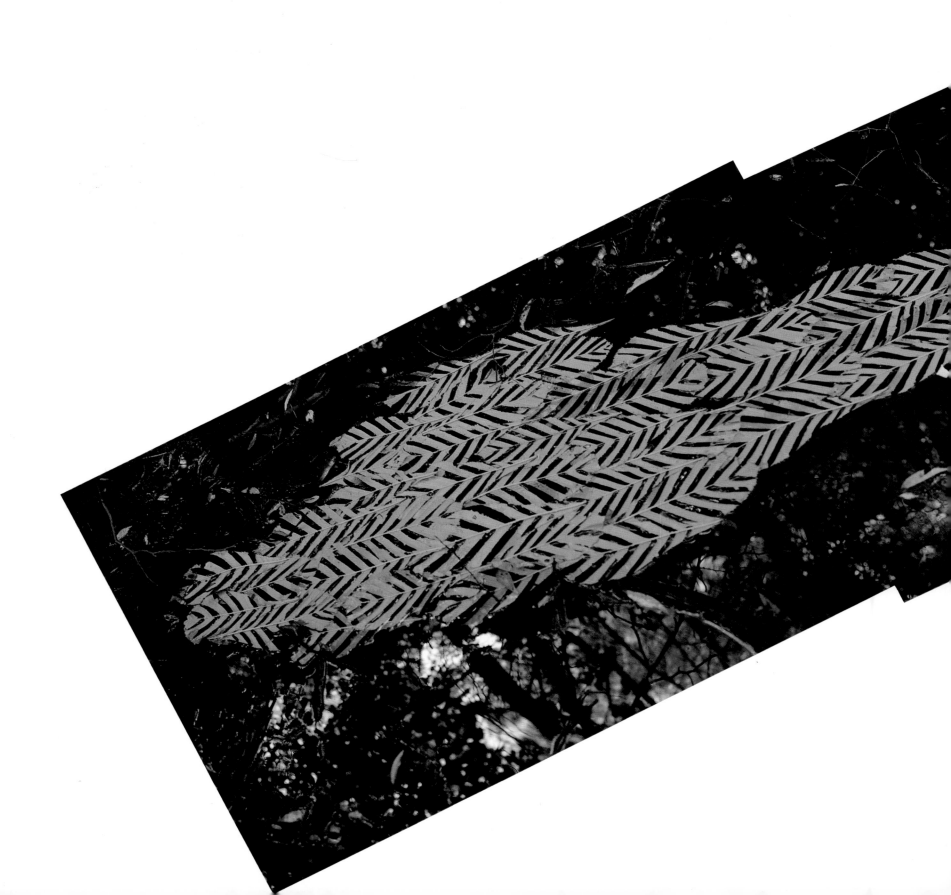

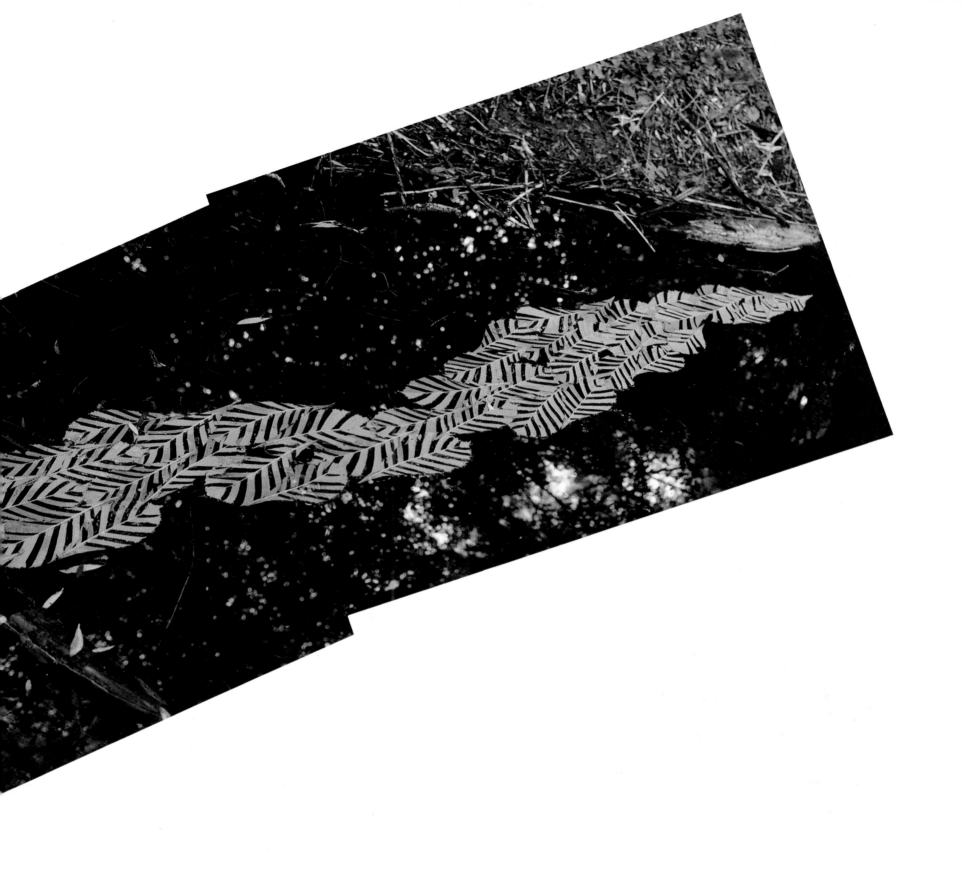

Horse chestnut leaves
sections torn out
pinned with thorns to sticks pushed into pond bottom
muddy black clouds stirred up around where I worked
over the week leaves fell and pond rose slightly
work gradually disappeared

LOUGHBOROUGH, LEICESTERSHIRE
22 SEPTEMBER 1986

Japanese maple
leaves stitched together to make a floating chain
the next day it became a hole
supported underneath by a woven briar ring

OUCHIYAMA-MURA, JAPAN
21-22 NOVEMBER 1987

Sycamore leaves
stitched together with stalks
hung from a tree

POLLOK PARK, GLASGOW
31 OCTOBER 1986

Iris and laurel leaves
stitched with thorns
two leaves thick
leaving a single layer of leaves for the light

CASTRES, FRANCE
23 & 25 OCTOBER 1988

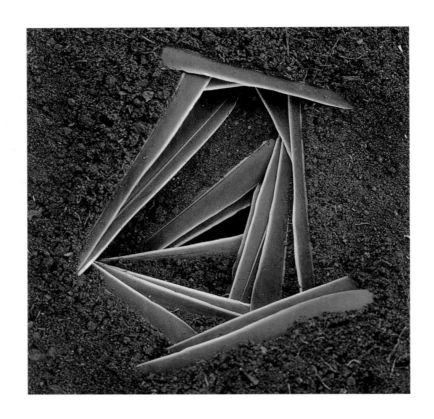

Wood pigeon wing feathers
partly buried
laid around a hole

LEEDS, YORKSHIRE
AUGUST 1977

Sycamore leaves

LEEDS, YORKSHIRE
SEPTEMBER 1977

Broken pebbles
scratched white with another stone

ST ABBS, THE BORDERS
I JUNE 1985

Broken icicle
reconstructed
spit welded
only able to work in the mornings when temperature below freezing
stored overnight in a sheep shelter

LANGHOLM, DUMFRIESSHIRE
22-23 FEBRUARY 1986

Leaves
polished, creased
made in the shadow of the tree from which they fell
pinned to the ground with thorns

LE JARDIN MASSEY, TARBES, FRANCE
22 AUGUST 1989

Rhododendron leaves
creased to catch the hazy to bright light
held to the ground with thorns

YORKSHIRE SCULPTURE PARK, WEST BRETTON
11 FEBRUARY 1987

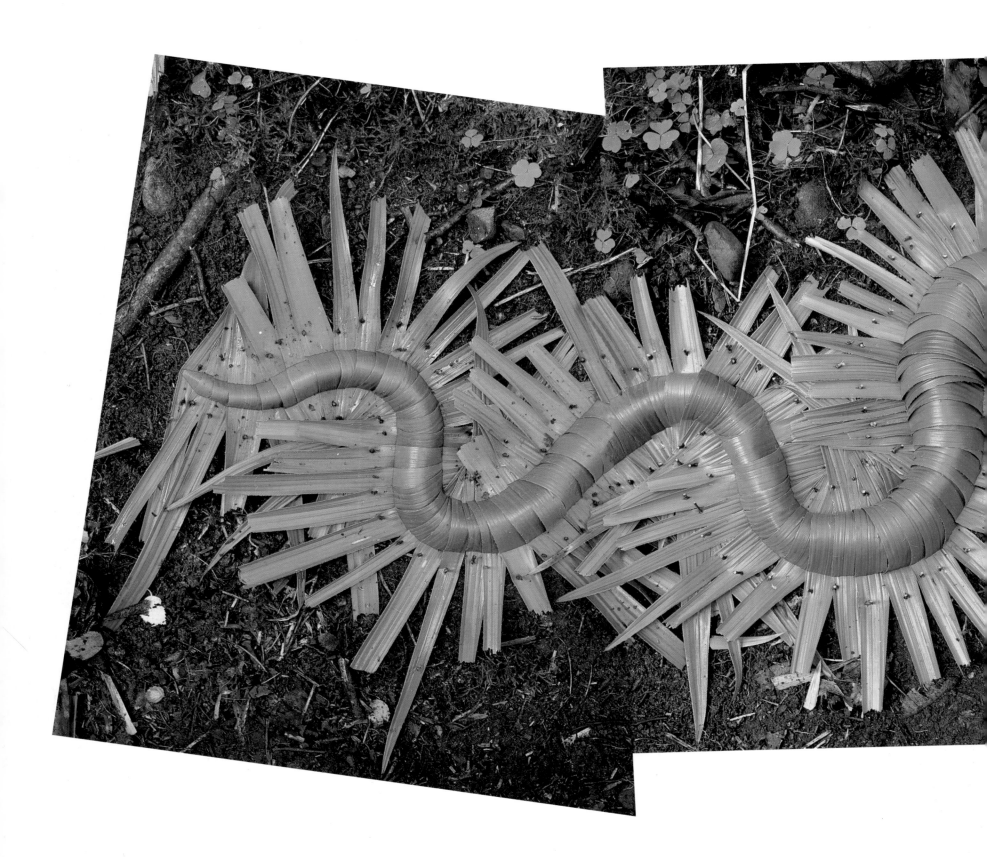

Blades of grass
creased and arched
secured with thorns

PENPONT, DUMFRIESSHIRE
14 AUGUST 1988

OVERLEAF

Snow and wind damaged pine trees
growing bent
thinned out
pinned together with metal rods
helped by students and friends

GRIZEDALE FOREST
SPRING 1985

Leadgate and Lambton earthworks
Excavator driver – Steve Fox

COUNTY DURHAM
WINTER-SPRING 1988-89

The wall

Stonework — Joe Smith

STONEWOOD, DUMFRIESSHIRE

1988-89

Sweet chestnut
autumn horn

PENPONT, DUMFRIESSHIRE
NOVEMBER 1986